MATTER

MATTER

EDITED BY ANDREA R. FIELD

Britannica
Educational Publishing
IN ASSOCIATION WITH

ROSEN
EDUCATIONAL SERVICES

Published in 2013 by Britannica Educational Publishing
(a trademark of Encyclopædia Britannica, Inc.)
in association with Rosen Educational Services, LLC
29 East 21st Street, New York, NY 10010.

First Edition

Britannica Educational Publishing
J.E. Luebering: Director, Core Reference Group, Encyclopædia Britannica
Adam Augustyn: Assistant Manager, Encyclopædia Britannica

Anthony L. Green: Editor, Compton's by Britannica
Michael Anderson: Senior Editor, Compton's by Britannica
Andrea R. Field: Senior Editor, Compton's by Britannica
Sherman Hollar: Associate Editor, Compton's by Britannica

Marilyn L. Barton: Senior Coordinator, Production Control
Steven Bosco: Director, Editorial Technologies
Lisa S. Braucher: Senior Producer and Data Editor
Yvette Charboneau: Senior Copy Editor
Kathy Nakamura: Manager, Media Acquisition

Rosen Educational Services
Jeanne Nagle: Senior Editor
Nelson Sá: Art Director
Cindy Reiman: Photography Manager
Karen Huang: Photo Researcher
Matthew Cauli: Designer, Cover Design
Introduction by Jeanne Nagle

Library of Congress Cataloging-in-Publication Data

Matter/edited by Andrea R. Field.—1st ed.
    p. cm.—(Introduction to physics)
"In association with Britannica Educational Publishing, Rosen Educational Services."
Includes bibliographical references and index.
ISBN 978-1-61530-839-2 (library binding)
1. Matter—Juvenile literature. I. Field, Andrea R.
QC173.16.M375 2013
530—dc23

2011052216

Manufactured in the United States of America

CONTENTS

INTRODUCTION 6

CHAPTER 1 THE BUILDING BLOCKS OF MATTER 10

CHAPTER 2 THE STATES OF MATTER 24

CHAPTER 3 INERTIA AND GRAVITATION 36

CHAPTER 4 THE EQUIVALENCE OF MATTER AND ENERGY 44

CHAPTER 5 OTHER MODERN THEORIES OF MATTER 52

CONCLUSION 65
GLOSSARY 68
FOR MORE INFORMATION 70
BIBLIOGRAPHY 73
INDEX 74

When dealing with physics, the answer to the question "What's the matter?" has to be a resounding "Everything!" The stars in the night sky, rocks found buried deep beneath Earth's surface, all creatures great and small (including humans)—everything and anything you can think of is composed of matter. This book takes that rather general statement and adds the details that explain the existence of matter, its properties, and, at the risk of stating the obvious, why matter ... "matters."

At the microscopic level, matter is made up of atoms, molecules, and ions. Close to 100 different types of atoms—the smallest pieces of matter—exist in nature. Molecules are combinations of atoms, while ions are single or grouped atoms that have an electrical charge. Clustered in the center of each atom are protons and neutrons, around which particles called electrons orbit.

There are three different forms, or phases, of matter: solid, liquid, and gas. Solid matter has a definite size and shape that does not change. The volume of liquids is definite, but their shape is determined by the container they occupy. Gases do not have a definite size or shape; they simply expand to fill a container completely. The phases of matter can change. One example is solid ice melting into liquid water; refreeze the water and you have a phase change in reverse.

Another characteristic of matter is that it is subject to inertia and gravitation. Inertia describes matter's resistance to stopping when it is moving and its resistance to moving when it is at rest. The more mass an object has—meaning the more matter the object is composed of—the greater the resistance. In other words, the more massive something is, the greater the force required to get it to move or stop moving.

Mass is not as important as weight when it comes to gravitation, or gravity, which is the force that attracts, or draws, all forms of matter to each other. On Earth, gravity pulls all objects toward the planet's core. An object's distance from the core determines the strength of this pull. Gravity, not mass, is what gives matter weight. For example, an object experiences a stronger gravitational pull at Earth's surface than it does at the top of a mountain. The strength of the pull, in turn, determines the object's weight. Thus,

Physicist John Dalton's table of elements, fronted by one of his diagrams of atoms and three atomic models.
Science and Society Picture Library/Getty Images

the object weighs more at the surface than it does atop the mountain, even though its mass has not changed.

People's understanding of matter has grown over the years. For centuries scientists were sure that matter and energy were two separate things. Yet, as Albert Einstein proved with his theory of special relativity (better known as $E=mc^2$), the two are so closely linked that they are said to be equivalent. In fact, matter can be converted to energy, and energy can be converted to matter.

Beyond special relativity, there have been other theories of matter raised in the modern era. The rise of quantum mechanics (the study of matter at the atomic and smaller levels), astronomical observations, and experimentation in particle physics each have revealed plenty about the nature of matter. No doubt more theories will come in the future as scientists continue to investigate the fundamental topic of matter.

CHAPTER 1

THE BUILDING BLOCKS OF MATTER

An electron, a grain of sand, an elephant, and a giant star at the edge of the visible universe all have one thing in common—they are composed of matter, which is the material substance that makes up the physical universe. A beam of light, the motion of a falling stone, and the explosion of a stick of dynamite also have one thing in common—they are expressions of energy. Together, energy and matter form the basis for all observable phenomena.

Matter is made up of tiny units known as atoms, molecules, and ions. Atoms are the basic building blocks of chemistry. An atom is the smallest piece of matter that has the characteristic properties of a chemical element, such as hydrogen, oxygen, calcium, iron, gold, and neon. More than 90 types of atoms exist in nature, and each one forms a different element. Though elements are made up of only

Water filling a glass beaker. A huge number of water molecules, not to mention hydrogen and oxygen atoms, are needed to fill a container such as this. iStockphoto/ Thinkstock

one type of atom—gold contains only gold atoms, and neon contains only neon atoms— other substances are mixtures of different kinds of atoms. Atoms also join together chemically to form molecules. Ions are electrically charged atoms or groups of atoms. All atoms are roughly the same size. About 50 million atoms of solid matter lined up in a row would measure only 0.4 inch (1 centimeter).

Since atoms, molecules, and ions are very small, the bulk matter of everyday life consists of large amounts of these components. A glass of water, for instance, contains an extremely large amount (about 8×10^{24}) of water molecules. Each water molecule is in turn made up of two hydrogen atoms and one oxygen atom that have been combined chemically.

ATOMS

Scientists long believed that atoms were "elementary particles" that had no discernible structure and could not be broken apart. In fact, the word "atom" comes from a Greek word meaning "indivisible." Since the end of the 19th century, however, it has been known that atoms are themselves made up of smaller particles. It requires a great deal of energy to break an atom into its component parts.

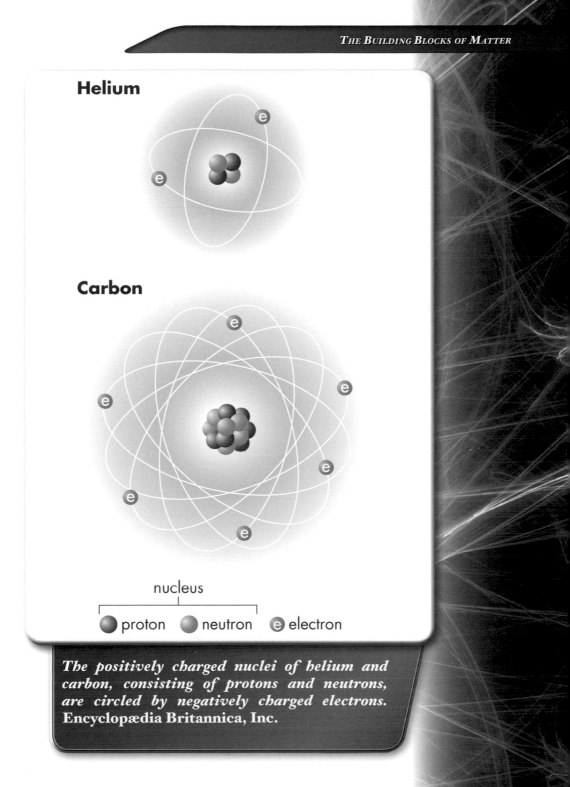

The positively charged nuclei of helium and carbon, consisting of protons and neutrons, are circled by negatively charged electrons. Encyclopædia Britannica, Inc.

Splitting the core of an atom involves nuclear reactions rather than ordinary chemical reactions.

PARTS OF THE ATOM

Atoms are made up of three basic types of particle: protons, neutrons, and electrons. These particles (as well as other particles smaller than atoms) are known as subatomic particles. Most of an atom consists of empty space. Its mass is concentrated in its center, which is called the nucleus. The nucleus consists of protons and neutrons. (The ordinary hydrogen atom is an exception; it contains one proton but no neutrons.) As their names suggest, protons have a positive electrical charge, while neutrons are electrically neutral—they carry no charge. Overall, then, the nucleus has a positive charge.

The number of protons determines which element is represented, while the number of neutrons determines which isotope of the element is represented. Isotopes are atoms of the same element that vary in mass because of differing numbers of neutrons.

Circling the nucleus is a cloud of electrons, which are negatively charged.

ELECTRICAL CHARGE AND IONS

It is the electrical forces in an atom that hold the atom together. Because opposite electric charges attract each other, there is an attractive force between the negatively charged

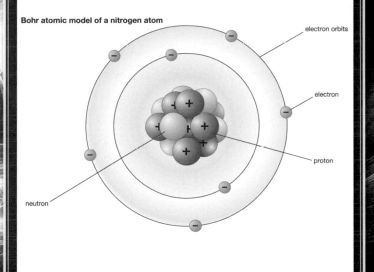

Bohr atomic model of a nitrogen atom

electron orbits

electron

proton

neutron

Electrons can circle the nucleus of an atom only in particular orbits of fixed size and energy. The Danish physicist Niels Bohr proposed this model of the atom in the early 20th century to explain how electrons can have stable orbits. Encyclopædia Britannica, Inc.

electrons and the positively charged protons. This force is what keeps the electrons in orbit around the nucleus, something like the way that gravity keeps Earth in orbit around the Sun. Unlike planets orbiting the Sun, however, electrons cannot be at any arbitrary distance from the nucleus. They can exist only in certain specific locations called allowed orbits.

Ordinarily, an atom has the same number of electrons and protons, each with an electrical charge of the same size. The negatively charged electrons and positively charged protons thus cancel each other out overall, so the atom as a whole is electrically neutral. Sometimes, however, an atom gains or loses electrons. It then becomes either negatively or positively charged and is called an ion.

The number of electrons determines an element's charge. Electrons are the lightest charged particles in nature: each has a mass of only about 9.1×10^{-28} gram. Protons and neutrons are about 1,836 times more massive. In fact, the nucleus accounts for 99.9 percent of the atom's mass, though it takes up a very small fraction of the atom's size. It constitutes only about 1/100,000 of the volume of the atom, about the same proportion as a marble to a football field. The nucleus is thus extremely dense.

Protons, neutrons, and electrons are long-lived particles present in ordinary, naturally occurring atoms. Other subatomic particles may be found in association with these three types of particles. They can be created only with the addition of enormous amounts of energy, however, and are very short-lived. In addition, protons and neutrons are themselves made up of smaller particles known as quarks. Electrons and quarks cannot be reduced or separated into smaller components, so they are considered elementary particles.

BASIC PROPERTIES

Each chemical element has a different number of protons in its atoms. A hydrogen atom, the simplest and lightest atom, has one proton. A helium atom has two protons; a carbon atom has six; and a silver atom has 47. Uranium, the heaviest element that occurs naturally in significant amounts, has 92 protons per atom. Scientists have assigned each element an atomic number, which is equal to the number of protons in the atom's nucleus. Hydrogen has atomic number 1, helium 2, and carbon 6.

An ordinary atom (rather than an ion) has the same number of electrons as protons. The atomic number thus also identifies the number of electrons in that atom. The number and arrangement of the electrons determine how one atom interacts with another. For this reason, the atomic number reveals the atom's chemical behavior.

The nuclei of a given element all have the same number of protons but may have different numbers of neutrons. Nuclei of an element that has different numbers of neutrons are said to be isotopes of each other. For example, about 99.8 percent of the oxygen nuclei in nature contain eight neutrons as well as eight protons. However, a very few oxygen nuclei contain nine neutrons and eight protons, and some even contain 10 neutrons and eight protons. Each kind of nucleus is a different isotope of oxygen.

Most hydrogen atoms are made up of a single proton with an electron circling it. However, one isotope of hydrogen, called deuterium, contains a neutron as well. An extremely rare form of hydrogen, called tritium, has one proton and two neutrons in its

THREE OXYGEN ISOTOPES

oxygen 16   oxygen 17   oxygen 18

A diagram represents the nuclei of three oxygen isotopes. Each nucleus has eight protons (gray) and eight, nine, or 10 neutrons (green). Encyclopædia Britannica, Inc.

nucleus. This is an unstable arrangement, so the tritium nucleus is radioactive. Over time it gives off a negatively charged particle and changes to a stable helium nucleus with two protons and one neutron.

Many other isotopes of the various elements are radioactive. They can give off radiation of different kinds, changing to other elements or to different isotopes of the same element. Many radioactive isotopes are man-made. They are produced in nuclear reactors or machines called particle accelerators. Also known as atom smashers, particle accelerators produce beams of fast-moving, electrically charged particles and cause them to collide. These collisions often cause new particles to form.

In addition to the 92 naturally occurring elements, scientists have synthesized more than two dozen others. (Two of these synthesized elements were later found to exist in nature but only in trace amounts.) All of these elements are unstable and decay radioactively; many of them exist for only a fraction of a second.

COMPOUNDS AND MIXTURES

Substances that are composed of more than one kind of atom are either compounds or mixtures. The atoms in compounds have undergone a chemical change and have joined together. This chemical bonding is the result of the force of attraction of the electrons of one atom for the nucleus of another atom or of the electrical forces between ions.

In one type of compound, atoms join together to form molecules. Molecules form

A particle accelerator in a French hospital. Such machines smash atoms together to create radioactive isotopes, which can be used for the diagnosis and treatment of cancer and other illnesses. **Alain Denantes/Gamma-Rapho/Getty Images**

when two or more atoms share electrons, resulting in what is called a covalent bond. These bonds are very strong and require a good deal of energy to break. Two atoms of hydrogen and one atom of oxygen can share electrons, for example, and form a water molecule. The chemical symbol for water, H_2O, denotes this combination. It is possible for

Table salt is a compound of sodium and chloride, which bond by exchanging an electron. Aaron Amat/Shutterstock.com

the same atoms to combine in different but definite proportions to form different molecules. For instance, two atoms of hydrogen can chemically bond with two atoms of oxygen to form a molecule of hydrogen peroxide (H_2O_2).

In another type of compound, atoms exchange an electron to form a bond called an ionic bond. These bonds are strong because the atoms have become more stable as a result of either losing or gaining an electron (called ionization). An example is sodium chloride (NaCl), or common table salt. Sodium gives up an electron and becomes positively charged (Na+) when heated in the presence of chlorine. The chlorine acquires this electron, becoming negatively charged (Cl-). The resulting compound consists of sodium ions and chloride ions arranged in a particular pattern.

Unlike in a compound, the atoms, molecules, or ions in a mixture intermingle with one another but are not joined chemically. Salt water is a kind of mixture called a solution. Salt is composed of ions, and they spread throughout the water when the salt dissolves.

CHAPTER 2

THE STATES
OF MATTER

Most of the matter that people ordinarily observe can be classified into one of three states, or phases: solid, liquid, or gas. Solid matter

Physical states

increasing energy

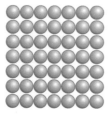

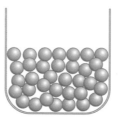

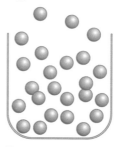

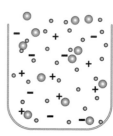

Solid

The molecules that make up a solid are arranged in regular, repeating patterns. They are held firmly in place but can vibrate within a limited area.

Liquid

The molecules that make up a liquid flow easily around one another. They are kept from flying apart by attractive forces between them. Liquids assume the shape of their containers.

Gas

The molecules that make up a gas fly in all directions at great speeds. They are so far apart that the attractive forces between them are insignificant.

Plasma

At the very high temperatures of stars, atoms lose their electrons. The mixture of electrons and nuclei that results is the plasma state of matter.

Physical states of matter. Encyclopædia Britannica, Inc

generally possesses and retains a definite size and shape, no matter where it is situated. A pencil, for example, does not change in size or shape if it is moved from a desktop and placed upright in a glass. A liquid, unlike a solid, assumes the shape of its container, even though, like a solid, it has a definite size, or volume. A pint of water changes its shape when it is poured from a glass into a bowl, but its volume remains the same. A gas expands to fill the complete volume of its container.

SOLIDS, LIQUIDS, AND GASES

At a given temperature and pressure, a substance will be in the solid, liquid, or gaseous state. But if the temperature or pressure changes, its state may also change. At constant atmospheric pressure the state of water, for example, changes with changes in temperature. Ice is water in the solid state. If it is removed from a freezer and placed in a warm pan, the ice warms up and changes to its liquid form—water. If the pan is then placed over a hot fire, the water heats up and changes to the gaseous state of water—steam.

Most substances can exist in any of the three states. Oxygen must be cooled to very

solid (ice)

liquid (water)

gas (steam)

The three most familiar states of matter are solid, liquid, and gas. Water exists in these states as ice, liquid water, and steam. Encyclopædia Britannica, Inc.

low temperatures before it becomes a liquid or a solid. Quartz must be heated to very high temperatures before it becomes a liquid or a gas.

In most people's experience, wide changes in pressure are not as common as drastic changes in temperature. For this reason, examples of the effects of pressure on the states of matter are not common. Often, high-pressure machines and vacuum (low-pressure) machines must be used to study the effects of pressure changes on matter. Under very low pressures, matter generally tends to enter the gaseous phase. At very high pressures gases

Travelers cooking a meal in the Mongolian mountains. Because of decreased air pressure at high elevations, water boils at lower temperatures. Thus, foods cooked by boiling cook at lower temperatures and take longer to cook. **Melissa McManus/Stone/Getty Images**

THE FOURTH STATE OF MATTER

At extremely high temperatures atoms may collide with such force that electrons are knocked free. The resulting mixture of free negative and positive particles is not a gas according to the usual definition. Such material is called a plasma.

The clouds of gas and dust called the Heart and Soul Nebulae, like most of interstellar space, are made of plasma. NASA/JPL-Caltech/UCLA

Some scientists consider plasma to be a fourth state of matter. Actually, about 99 percent of the known matter in the universe is in the plasma state. In stars matter is hot enough, and in interstellar space it is diffuse enough, for the electrons to be completely separated from the nuclei. From an astronomical standpoint, somewhat unusual conditions exist on Earth, where plasmas are difficult to produce.

tend to liquefy and liquids tend to solidify. In fact, at the very lowest temperatures that can be reached, helium will not solidify unless a pressure of some 25 times normal atmospheric pressure is applied.

The relation between pressure and temperature in changes of state is familiar to people who live at high altitudes. There the pressure is lower than at sea level, so water boils at a lower temperature. Cooking anything in water takes longer on a mountaintop than at sea level.

ATOMIC THEORY AND THE STATES OF MATTER

Regardless of whether water is in the solid, liquid, or gaseous state, its molecules always consist of one atom of oxygen and two atoms of hydrogen. Solid water, liquid water, and gaseous water all have the same chemical composition. Instead, the difference between these physical states depends on which energy is larger, the energy associated with the attraction between molecules or the heat energy.

A certain amount of attraction exists between all molecules. If repulsive forces are weaker than these intermolecular attractive forces, the molecules stick together. However, molecules are in constant random motion because of their thermal, or heat, energy. As the temperature of a substance increases, this molecular motion becomes greater. The molecules spread out and are less likely to unite. As the temperature decreases, the motion becomes smaller. The molecules are thus more likely to linger in each other's vicinity and bind together.

In a solid, the intermolecular attractive forces overcome the disruptive thermal energies of the molecules. In most solids the molecules are bound together in a rigid, orderly arrangement called a crystal. These types of solids are called crystalline solids. (In some other solids, such as glasses, gels, and many plastics, the molecules are not

The crystalline sparkle of snowflakes. Though held in a rigid pattern, all of the snow flakes and other crystals are actually vibrating. Terric Delayn/ Shutterstock.com

arranged in crystals.) Although the molecules in a crystal are held rigidly in place, they still vibrate because of their thermal energy. It may be difficult to think of ice as having heat energy. But even in ice each water molecule, though held firmly in the crystal pattern, vibrates around a fixed position. This vibrational motion is an expression of the thermal energy of ice.

As the temperature of the solid is increased, its molecules vibrate with greater and greater energies. Eventually, they gain enough vibrational energy to overcome the intermolecular attractive forces. They then break loose from their fixed positions in the crystal arrangement and move about more or less freely. The substance now assumes the shape of its container but maintains a constant volume. In other words, the substance has melted and is now a liquid.

PHASE CHANGES

Melting is a change of state, or a phase change. In melting, a solid changes to a liquid. The temperature at which melting takes place varies from substance to substance. Water and iron, for example, melt at different temperatures. The melting temperature is the same, however, for a given material at a given pressure. At atmospheric pressure water always melts at 32° F (0° C).

Phase changes can work in reverse. If the temperature of a liquid is gradually decreased, a point is eventually reached at which the intermolecular forces are strong enough to bind the molecules despite the disruptive thermal motions. Then a crystal forms; the substance has frozen. The temperature at which this liquid-to-solid phase change takes place is the freezing point. The freezing point of a substance occurs at the same temperature as its melting point.

This theory of matter can also explain the liquid-to-gas change of state, a process called vaporization or evaporation. As heat is applied to a liquid, some molecules gain sufficient thermal energy to overcome the surface tension, or the intermolecular attraction exerted by molecules at the surface of the liquid. These high-energy molecules break free from the liquid and move away. Such molecules are now in the gaseous state. As more heat is applied, more molecules gain enough energy to move away. Finally, at a temperature called the boiling point of the liquid, all the molecules can gain enough energy to escape from the liquid state.

The average distance between molecules in the gaseous state is extremely large compared to the size of the molecules. For this reason, the intermolecular forces in a gas are quite weak. This explains why a gas fills

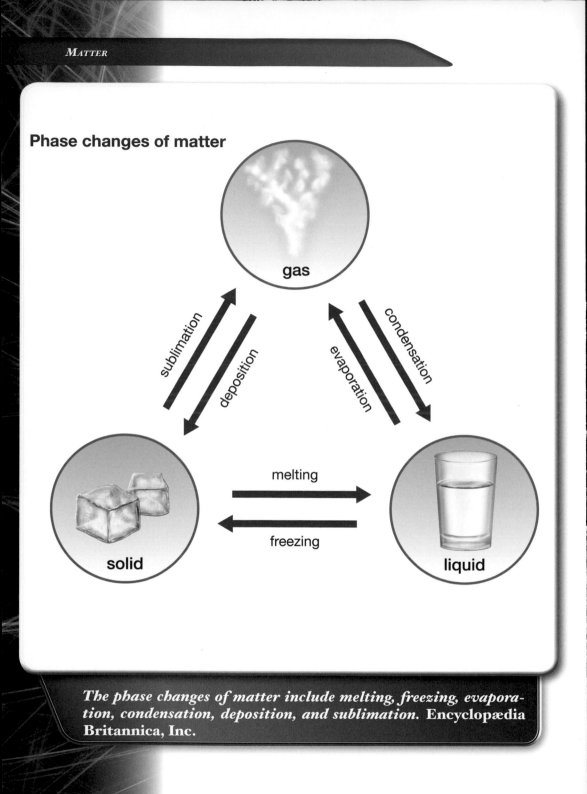

Phase changes of matter

The phase changes of matter include melting, freezing, evaporation, condensation, deposition, and sublimation. Encyclopædia Britannica, Inc.

the entire volume of its container. Since the intermolecular forces are so small, a gas molecule moves until it strikes either another gas molecule or the container wall. The overall effect of the many molecules striking the container walls is observed as pressure.

Sometimes a substance will pass directly from the solid state to the gaseous state without passing through the liquid state. This process is called sublimation. Dry ice (solid carbon dioxide) sublimates at atmospheric pressure. Liquid carbon dioxide can form if the gas is subjected to over five times atmospheric pressure.

CHAPTER 3

INERTIA AND GRAVITATION

A nother way of approaching the subject of matter is based on the concepts of inertia and gravitation. Matter can be defined as anything that has inertia and experiences an attractive force when in a gravitational field.

INERTIA

In the 17th century the great physicist Sir Isaac Newton formulated three basic laws of motion. The first law describes inertia, a fundamental property of all matter. It states that a body at rest tends to remain at rest, while a body in motion tends to keep on moving at the same speed and in a straight line. In order to move a resting body or to stop a moving body, some effort, called a force, is required. The tendency of a body to remain at rest or, once moving, to remain in motion is inertia. In other words, inertia is the property of a body through which it resists attempts to change its state of motion.

A man pushing against a boulder on a stony Russian beach. More force is required to overcome inertia in the massive boulder than in the smaller stones, which have less mass. Borge Ousland/National Geographic Image Collection/Getty Images

The inertia of a body is related to its mass. In fact, mass is defined as the measure of a body's inertia. More massive bodies possess greater inertia than less massive bodies. It is much more difficult to push a giant boulder that is sitting on the ground than a resting pebble. More force is required to overcome the boulder's greater inertia. The boulder thus has a greater mass than the pebble.

Galileo and Inertia

The principle of inertia is the starting point of the branch of physics known as classical mechanics. Although this principle can seem simple, it is actually not obvious to the untrained eye. In ordinary experience, objects that are not being pushed tend to come to rest.

The law of inertia was deduced in the 17th century by Galileo from his experiments with balls rolling down slanted planes. He noticed that if a ball rolled down one plane and up another, it would seek to regain its initial height above the ground, regardless of the inclines of the two planes. That meant that if the second plane were not inclined at all but were horizontal, the ball, unable to regain its original height, would keep rolling forever. A body moving horizontally would tend to stay in motion unless something interfered with it.

For Galileo, the principle of inertia was fundamental to his central scientific task: to explain how it is possible that if Earth is really spinning on its axis and orbiting the Sun we do not sense that motion. The principle of inertia helps to provide the answer. Since we are in motion together with Earth, and our natural tendency is to retain that motion, Earth appears to us to be at rest.

In the Newtonian formulation of the principle of inertia, the common observation that bodies that are not pushed tend to come to

An antique spinning globe. The principle of inertia explains how Earth can spin but the motion is undetectable. iStockphoto/Thinkstock

rest is attributed to the fact that they actually have forces acting on them to cause them to stop moving. Friction and air resistance, for instance, are forces that can cause a moving body to slow down and eventually stop. A ball rolling on the ground rubs against the ground and the molecules of the surrounding air. This works to bring it to rest.

A body's mass can be measured by exerting a force on the body and measuring the acceleration that results. Newton's second law of motion states that the mass (m) is equal to the force (F) divided by the acceleration (a): $m = F/a$.

In principle, this measurement can be made anywhere in the universe. Wherever the experiment is performed, the same force applied to the same body produces the same acceleration. The mass of a body is, therefore, the same everywhere.

GRAVITATION

All matter exerts a gravitational attractive force on other matter. The gravitational force is weak compared to the three other known forces—the electromagnetic force, the strong force (which holds the nucleus of an atom together), and the weak force (which is involved in some forms of radioactivity). The magnetic force of a small magnet, for example, can hold up a pin against the gravitational pull of the entire Earth. However, on the scale of everyday objects near Earth or that of astronomical bodies, the gravitational force is the dominant one of the four

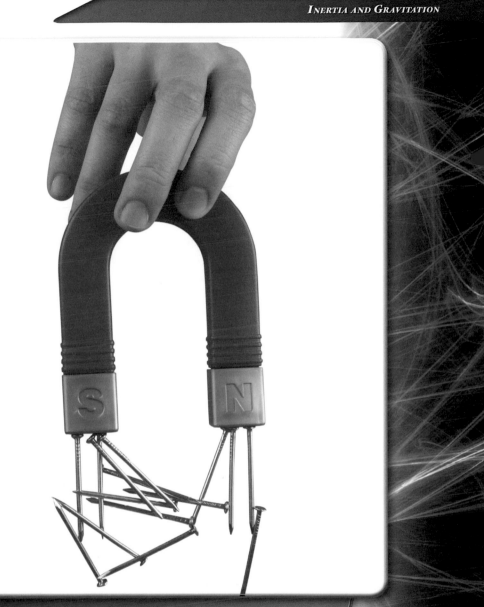

A hand magnet attracting nails. Gravitation is such a weak force that a magnet is able to overcome the gravitational pull of Earth. © www.istockphoto. com/ Matthew Cole

known forces. The fall of bodies released from a height to the surface of Earth is the most familiar example of gravitation. Earth's orbit around the Sun and the motion of the Sun are also results of the force of gravitation.

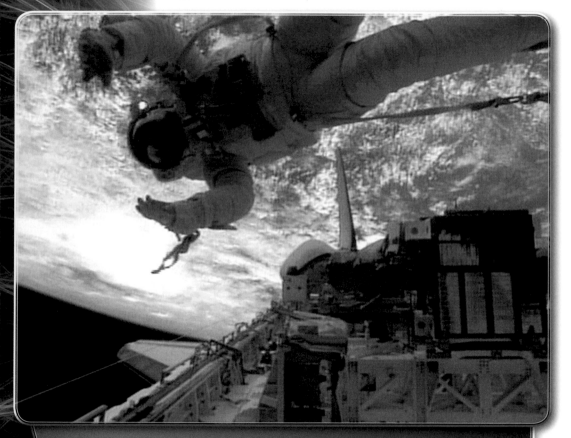

An astronaut is moved by the robotic arm of the space shuttle Endeavour during a space walk in 1995. Although gravity still exists in space, astronauts do not feel it because they are in a state that scientists call free-fall. As a result, the astronauts experience a feeling of weightlessness, or floating. © **AP Images**

The weight of a body is determined by the gravitational forces exerted upon it. A body at Earth's surface experiences a gravitational pull toward the center of the planet. If the body moves farther from Earth's center—to the top of a high mountain, for example—the gravitational force on it decreases, so its weight decreases. If the body moves to a lower point—into a deep valley, for example—the gravitational force on it increases, so its weight increases. The increase is far greater if the body then moves to the gravitational field of a giant planet, say, Jupiter. A body's weight can change; it varies with the strength of the gravitational field in which the body is placed.

It is important to understand the difference between mass and weight. While the mass of a body is the same everywhere, the weight of a body depends upon the strength of the local gravitational field. An astronaut standing on the surface of the Moon weighs less than he does when standing on Earth, but his mass is the same in both places.

However, there is a relationship between mass and weight. Mass and weight are proportional to each other. The more mass a body has, the more it will weigh at any given point in space.

CHAPTER 4

THE EQUIVALENCE OF MATTER AND ENERGY

I n the early 20th century Albert Einstein developed the theory of special relativity. This theory, which considers matter and energy equivalent, greatly extended

Albert Einstein's theory of special relativity revolutionized the study of physics and scientific understanding of the nature of matter. **AFP/Getty Images**

scientists' understanding of matter. It states that anything having energy has mass and that the amount of a body's mass (*m*) is related to the amount of its energy (*E*). The exact relationship is given by Einstein's famous equation, $E = mc^2$, where *c* is the speed of light—186,300 miles per second (3×10^8 meters per second).

THE SURPRISING VARIABILITY OF MASS

The theory of special relativity was revolutionary and difficult for many to accept.

Jets at an airport in Las Vegas. The motion of the jet that is taking off adds an imperceptible amount of mass, while the stationary aircraft have stable rest mass. **Christopher Parypa/Shutterstock.com**

Scientists had been accustomed to viewing matter and energy as two separate quantities of the universe. But the theory of special relativity relates the two. According to this theory, an object's mass varies as its speed changes. An object traveling at a high velocity will have a greater mass than the same object traveling at a low velocity. The smallest mass a body can have is the mass it has when it is at rest. This minimum mass is called the body's rest mass, and it never changes.

Even at speeds that are ordinarily regarded as quite high—the speed of a jet aircraft, for example—the increase in mass from the rest mass is too small to detect. But in high-energy particle accelerators, when a particle travels at speeds near the speed of light, the mass of the particle increases observably.

THE CONSERVATION OF MASS AND ENERGY

Centuries of experiments had led scientists to believe that the amount of matter in the universe never changes. They expressed this concept as the law of the conservation of mass: Matter can neither be created nor destroyed. Similar to this law is the law of the conservation of energy, which states that energy can neither be created nor destroyed. One reason that Einstein's theory of relativity was so hard to accept was that it said these laws were wrong, that energy can be converted to matter and that matter can be converted to energy. Experimental observations have since confirmed this fact.

Conversion of Matter to Energy

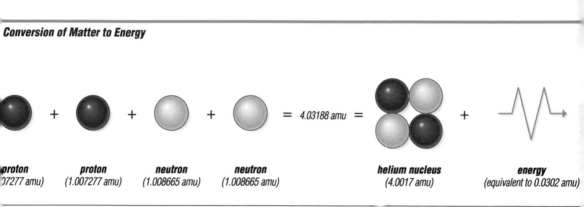

| proton
(1.007277 amu) | proton
(1.007277 amu) | neutron
(1.008665 amu) | neutron
(1.008665 amu) | = 4.03188 amu = | helium nucleus
(4.0017 amu) | energy
(equivalent to 0.0302 amu) |

The sum of masses of two protons and two neutrons is 4.03188 atomic mass units (amu). When they are joined in a helium nucleus, their mass is 0.0302 amu smaller. The difference has been converted into energy. The helium nucleus is very stable. **Encyclopaedia Britannica, Inc.**

The conversion of matter to energy can be demonstrated in nuclear reactions. The masses of individual protons and neutrons are frequently measured in atomic mass units (amu). One amu is 1/12 of the mass of an atom of carbon-12 (the most common form of carbon). The mass of a free proton is 1.007277 amu. The mass of a free neutron is slightly larger: 1.008665 amu. When two protons and two neutrons join to form a helium nucleus, one might expect that the mass of the helium nucleus would be equal to the sum of the masses of two protons and two neutrons, or 4.03188 amu. But experiments show that a helium nucleus has a mass of 4.0017 amu, or 0.0302 less than their sum. The missing 0.0302 amu was converted to energy.

The helium nucleus has less energy than its isolated components. That energy difference contributes to the stability of the helium nucleus and is called its binding energy. The exact amount of energy that was given up in forming the helium nucleus must be supplied to break it up, that is, to overcome the binding energy.

Matter also changes to energy in chemical reactions, when atoms or molecules are formed. However, the amount of mass converted to energy is much smaller than in a nuclear reaction and is not observed.

Experiments have convinced scientists that mass and energy are equivalent and interchangeable. The laws of the conservation of mass and the conservation of energy have therefore been combined into a single law, the law of the conservation of mass-energy. This states that the sum of the mass and the energy in the universe is a constant. Transformations between mass and energy are governed by the equation $E = mc^2$.

RELATIVITY AND NUCLEAR PHYSICS

Among the outstanding advances in science will always stand Albert Einstein's theories of relativity — the problem of how physical laws and measurements change when considered by observers in various states of motion. These theories forced revision of all fundamental thinking about time and space. They brought changes in many statements of natural law, including Isaac Newton's law of gravitation. And the theories gave scientists the mathematical framework they needed for atomic research and for releasing atomic energy.

The explosive power of nuclear weapons comes from the conversion of mass to energy when atoms are either split apart or fused together. To Einstein's horror, during the late 1930s, physicists began seriously to consider whether his equation $E = mc^2$ might make an atomic bomb possible. In 1920 Einstein himself had considered but eventually dismissed the possibility. However, he left it open if a method could be found to magnify the power of the atom. Then in 1938–39 the scientists Otto Hahn, Fritz Strassmann, Lise Meitner, and Otto Frisch showed that vast amounts of energy could be unleashed by the splitting of the uranium atom. Through a process called nuclear fission, the nucleus of a heavy element such as uranium splits into two fragments of smaller total mass, with the mass difference released as energy.

This and other discoveries led to the first atomic bombs and reactors. In the years following World War II many uses were found for nuclear reactors, from nuclear-powered ships and submarines to nuclear power plants for generating electricity for public use. As powerful as the atomic bomb was, some scientists developed an even more deadly weapon—a nuclear fusion bomb (the hydrogen bomb), which was first tested in 1952.

Museum visitors examining replicas of the world's first two nuclear bombs, "Fat Man" (right) and "Little Boy." The conversion of mass to energy makes nuclear weapons possible. **Ben Martin/Time & Life Pictures/Getty Images**

CHAPTER 5

OTHER MODERN THEORIES OF MATTER

B asic ideas about matter trace back to Isaac Newton and even earlier to ancient Greece. Further understanding of matter, along with new puzzles, began emerging in the early 20th century. As we have seen, Einstein's theory of special relativity showed that matter and energy can be converted into each other.

The concept of matter was further complicated by the development of the branch of physics known as quantum mechanics, which studies matter and energy at the smallest scales. At the level of atoms and smaller particles, the behavior of matter and energy often seems peculiar. In the quantum view, elementary particles behave both like tiny balls and like waves that spread out in space—a seeming paradox that has yet to be fully resolved.

Additional complexity in the meaning of matter came from astronomical observations that began in the 1930s. These observations showed that a large fraction of the universe

Albert Einstein (left), *who developed the theory of special relativity, consults with Wolfgang Pauli, notable for his work in quantum mechanics. Relativity and quantum theory together form the theoretical foundations of modern physics.* **Science and Society Picture Library/ Getty Images**

consists of "dark matter." This invisible material does not affect light and can be detected only through its gravitational effects. Its detailed nature has yet to be determined.

PARTICLE AND WAVE PROPERTIES OF MATTER

Light is a form of energy. At the beginning of the 20th century, light was thought to consist of electromagnetic waves. In experiments beams of light overlap, scatter, and bend in patterns that are found only in waves. However, in 1905 Einstein showed that in certain circumstances light behaves as if it must consist of tiny particles, called photons. His findings created a great enigma for scientists: was light to be considered a wave or a particle? The surprising answer is both. The particle aspects and the wave aspects of light complement each other. Both are necessary for a complete understanding of light.

It was long known that matter, on the other hand, behaves as if it is composed of particles. In 1923 Louis de Broglie advanced the hypothesis that matter might also exhibit the properties of waves. Four years later "matter waves" were actually observed.

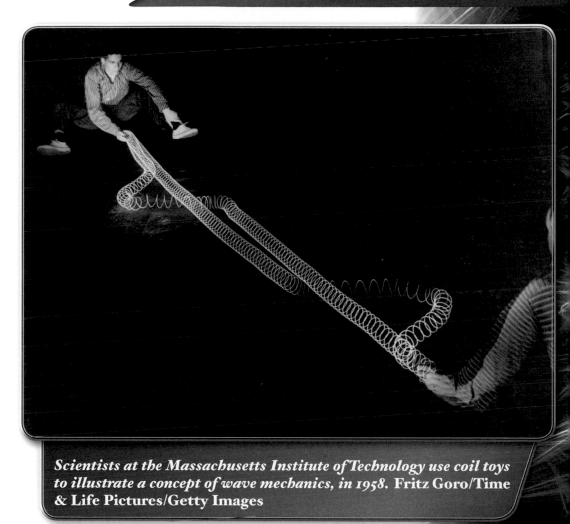

Scientists at the Massachusetts Institute of Technology use coil toys to illustrate a concept of wave mechanics, in 1958. **Fritz Goro/Time & Life Pictures/Getty Images**

Beams of electrons were aimed at crystals, and their patterns of scattering were observed. These patterns looked as if they had been formed by waves, confirming the theory that electrons could act like waves. In

Louis de Broglie, wave mechanics pioneer, in the 1930s. Science and Society Picture Library/Getty Images.

similar experiments atoms, molecules, neutrons, protons, and many other particles of
matter were shown to behave like waves. As
strange as this finding seems, at the smallest
scales matter does have properties of both
particles and waves.

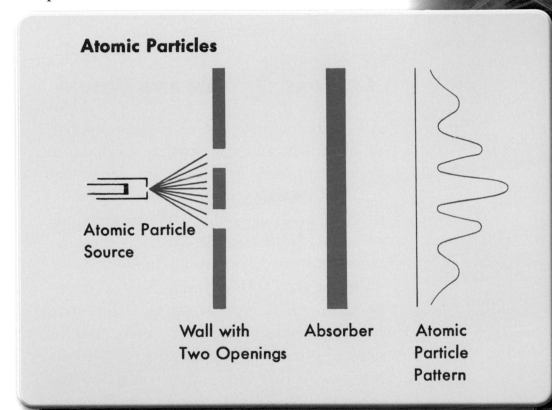

Atomic Particles

Atomic Particle
Source

Wall with
Two Openings

Absorber

Atomic
Particle
Pattern

*In this experiment, electrons are shot through a wall with double
slits. The slits are so narrow that gaps between atoms in crystals must
be used. The pattern is of electrons on the absorber, shown at right,
like one associated with wave phenomena. (In actual experiments
the pattern is more complicated than shown here.)* **Encyclopædia
Britannica, Inc.**

Electron waves are used to great advantage in the electron microscope. Because the waves are much shorter than light waves or even ultraviolet waves, the electron microscope has a much greater resolving power than light microscopes. Electron microscopes show much more detail than do light microscopes.

LEPTONS, QUARKS, AND BOSONS

All matter is made up of elementary particles, which cannot be further divided into component parts. Atoms are not elementary particles since they are themselves composed of smaller particles—electrons, protons, and neutrons. Some particles, such as photons, commonly exist apart from atoms.

In the early 20th century scientists developed methods for studying radioactive particles, for breaking atoms apart, and for detecting particles from space called cosmic rays. As they did so, they concluded that other particles besides the photon, electron, proton, and neutron must exist. In order to account for a type of radioactive decay, in the 1930s Wolfgang Pauli and Enrico Fermi postulated the neutrino, a particle with no electrical charge and either very little or

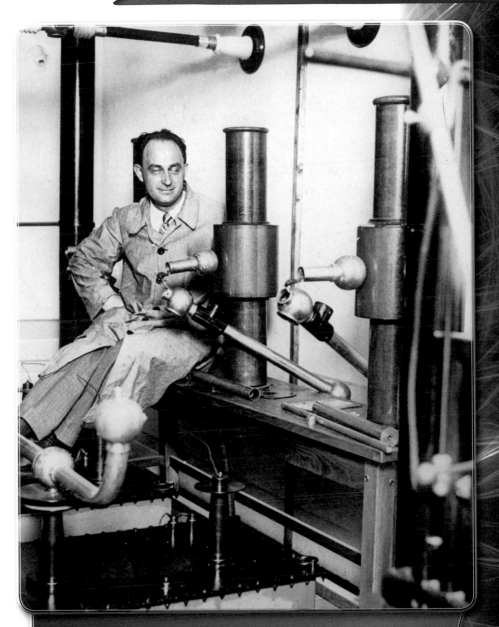

Physicist Enrico Fermi. His work investigating subatomic particles helped usher in the nuclear age. **Imagno/Hulton Archive/Getty Images**

no mass. It interacts much more weakly with matter than a photon does. Particles with the characteristics predicted by Pauli and Fermi were very difficult to detect, but experiments performed in 1956 confirmed their existence.

Since then, hundreds of different types of subatomic particles have been detected as a result of collisions produced in cosmic-ray reactions and particle-accelerator experiments. Most of these particles are highly unstable, existing for less than a millionth of a second.

There are three different types of subatomic particle: leptons, quarks, and bosons. Leptons and quarks are thought to be true elementary particles. Together they form atoms, so they are considered the most fundamental building blocks of matter. The six known types of leptons are the electron, the muon, the tau, and the three types of neutrino. There are also six types of quark. Quarks make up neutrons and protons.

While leptons and quarks are "matter" particles, some bosons are "force" particles. They transmit the different types of forces and thus can be thought of as the cement that binds the building blocks of matter together. These bosons are also elementary particles. The most familiar boson is the photon, which carries the electromagnetic force.

DARK MATTER

In the 20th century a problem regarding galaxies of stars began to puzzle astronomers. Most, if not all, galaxies occur in clusters, presumably held together by the gravity of the cluster members. However, astronomers found that nearly all the galaxies are moving too fast to be held together only by the gravity of the matter that is visible. More matter must be present in order to keep the galaxies from flying apart.

This unseen matter was dubbed dark matter, and it exists in at least two forms. Some of it consists of well-understood objects such as undetected planets, brown dwarfs (bodies just short of having enough mass to become stars), neutron stars, and black holes. This type of dark matter is called baryonic. The other type of dark matter is "cold," meaning that its particles are moving slowly relative to each other. This cold dark matter is not made of protons and neutrons like ordinary matter.

It turns out that "ordinary" matter is actually less common—most of the matter in the universe is cold dark matter. All together, the different kinds of matter make up about 27 percent of the matter and energy in the universe. Visible matter accounts for only 0.5 percent of the universe. Baryonic dark matter makes up about another 4.5 percent of the matter-energy, while cold dark matter accounts for 22 percent.

ANTIMATTER

In 1928 the physicist P.A.M. Dirac claimed that a particle of the same mass as an electron but having a positive charge could exist. Four years later a positive elcctron, or positron, was detected. This was the first experimental

A worker operates a machine that produces antiprotons, a type of antimatter, at Fermi National Accelerator Laboratory in Illinois.
MCT via Getty Images

evidence for the existence of antimatter, which is composed of antiparticles. If a particle possesses an electrical charge, its antiparticle possesses the same mass and an equal but opposite charge. Numerous other kinds of antimatter particles have since been discovered. Particle physicists now assume that every

The Milky Way galaxy. Unlike other galaxies, the Milky Way is believed to be composed mainly of particles, rather than antiparticles. Sander van Sinttruye/ Shutterstock.com

subatomic particle has a corresponding anti-particle, even if the antiparticle has not yet been observed.

An important property of matter is demonstrated when an electron and a positron meet. In a small fraction of a second they annihilate, or destroy, one another—both particles disappear. The law of conservation of mass-energy states that if mass is destroyed, an equivalent amount of energy must be created. When an electron and a positron annihilate each other, this is indeed what happens. A large amount of energy, corresponding to the mass of the two particles, is always given off. Similar annihilations occur when other particles meet their antiparticles.

The Milky Way galaxy, to which Earth belongs, is apparently composed primarily of particles rather than antiparticles. It obviously cannot be made up of equal amounts of particles and antiparticles, for if it were there would be a cataclysmic annihilation and all the matter in the galaxy would be converted to energy. There is also no evidence that other galaxies in the universe are composed primarily of antiparticles. Matter apparently dominates antimatter in the universe, for reasons that are not yet fully understood.

Conclusion

S ince the early 20th century physicists have made great strides in understanding the nature of matter, yet many questions remain. For one thing, it has been difficult to develop a single theory of physics that can explain the behavior of matter on all scales. Relativity is essential for studying the universe on a large scale, when extremely high speeds or great densities are involved, and for understanding gravity. On the other hand, quantum mechanics is needed to study matter and energy at the smallest scales.

In an attempt to develop a unified theory, many physicists have turned to string theory. According to this theory, elementary particles are not dimensionless points but tiny one-dimensional string-like objects. Although these "strings" are so small that they appear to be points, they actually have a tiny length. If 1 billion trillion trillion of them were laid end to end, they would together be only about 0.4 inch (1 centimeter) long.

According to string theory, these strings make up all matter, and they vibrate. The particular pattern of a string's vibrations corresponds to a particular type of particle. The strings that form electrons all have one vibrational pattern, for instance, while those that form quarks have a different pattern, and photons yet another.

Although the mathematics of string theory has shown great promise, the theory has not yet been verified by experiment. Strings, if they exist, are extremely tiny. Physicists hope that the latest generation of particle accelerators will be able to detect such small objects. They are also seeking other ways to confirm string theory.

String theory might be a way to incorporate all types of matter and all four forces into one framework of physics. Such a comprehensive physical theory is known as a unified field theory or a "theory of everything." Meanwhile, other physicists have been taking different approaches in the attempt to find such a theory. The hunt also continues for the elusive Higgs boson, a theoretical particle that gives all matter its mass. Without such a particle, the standard model of physics cannot account for why different types of particles have widely different masses. So far, there is no experimental evidence that the Higgs boson exists, but physicists continue to search for it, using the most powerful particle accelerators available. If the Higgs boson does exist, its discovery would be crucial to a final understanding of the structure of matter.

boson Any of a group of subatomic particles that transmit various types of forces; the cement that binds matter together.

electron An elementary, negatively charged subatomic particle that orbits the nucleus of an atom.

gravitation The attractive force that draws matter together.

inertia A fundamental property of matter stating that a body at rest tends to remain at rest, while a body in motion tends to keep moving at the same speed and in a straight line.

intermolecular Carried on or occurring between or among molecules.

lepton Any member of a group of elementary subatomic particles that, along with quarks, form atoms.

molecule The smallest particle of a substance that retains all the properties of substance, composed of one or more atoms.

neutron A subatomic particle with no electric charge that is found in every atomic nucleus except those of ordinary hydrogen.

nucleus The center portion of an atom, made up of protons and (usually) neutrons.

paradox A statement, action, or situation that seems to contradict itself.

photon A subatomic particle that represents a portion of electromagnetic radiation.

plasma A mixture of free negative and positive particles that some scientists consider to be the fourth state of matter.

proton A positively charged subatomic particle that, together with neutrons, makes up all atomic nuclei except for the hydrogen nucleus (which consists of a single proton).

quantum Any of the very small increments or parcels into which energy, electric charge, or other physical properties are subdivided.

quark Any member of a group of elementary subatomic particles that, along with leptons, form atoms. Quarks make up protons and neutrons.

subatomic Of or relating to particles that are smaller than atoms.

velocity Quantity that designates how fast and in what direction an object is moving.

American Association for the Advancement
  of Science (AAAS)
1200 New York Avenue NW
Washington, DC 20005
(202) 326-6400
Web site: http://www.aaas.org
An international nonprofit organization,
  AAAS produces publications, hosts scientific conferences and meetings, and
  undertakes many programs and activities
  that promote all fields of science.

American Institute of Physics (AIP)
One Physics Ellipse
College Park, MD 20740
(301) 209-3100
Web site: http://www.aip.org
The AIP provides leadership to physical
  science societies across the nation, and
  also offers programs, publications, and
  outreach services within the field.

Canadian Association of Physicists (CAP)
Suite 112, MacDonald Building
University of Ottawa
150 Louis Pasteur Priv.
Ottawa, ON K1N 6N5
Canada
(613) 562-5614

Web site: http://www.cap.ca

Committed to advancing research and education in the field of physics, CAP supports a number of programs and resources for individuals pursuing physics-related careers. The organization also conducts lectures and sponsors competitions for students, as well as events for the general public.

The Franklin Institute
222 North 20th Street
Philadelphia, PA 19103
(215) 448-1200
Web site: http://www2.fi.edu

The Franklin Institute's collection of scientific artifacts and unique exhibits include hands-on activities demonstrating the various aspects of physics, as well as an extensive space inspired by the life and work of Isaac Newton.

National Science Foundation (NSF)
4201 Wilson Boulevard
Arlington, VA 22230
(703) 292-5111
Web site: http://www.nsf.gov

The NSF is an independent government agency that supports scientific research and advancement throughout the United States in a variety of fields, including physics and other physical sciences.

TRIUMF (Tri-University Meson Facility)
University of British Columbia
4004 Wesbrook Mall
Vancouver, BC, V6T 2A3
Canada
(604) 222-1047
Web site: http://www.triumf.ca
Canada's national laboratory for particle and nuclear physics, TRIUMF is the country's leader in exploring the structure and origins of matter. Outreach and educational opportunities include fellowships and master classes for high school science students, and a lecture series for the general public.

WEB SITES

Due to the changing nature of Internet links, Rosen Educational Services has developed an online list of Web sites related to the subject of this book. This site is updated regularly. Please use this link to access the list:

www.rosenlinks.com/inphy/matter

Bradley, David, and Ian Crofton. *Atoms and Elements* (Oxford Univ. Press, 2002).

Cooper, Christopher. *Matter* (DK, 2000).

Fleisher, Paul. *Matter and Energy*; Relativity and Quantum Mechanics (Lerner, 2009).

Gardner, Robert. *Science Fair Projects About the Properties of Matter, Revised and Expanded Using the Scientific Method* (Enslow, 2010).

Green, Dan. *Physics: Why Matter Matters!* (Kingfisher, 2010).

Jedicke, Peter. *Gravity, and How It Works* (Chelsea House, 2008).

Kirkland, Kyle. *Atoms and Materials* (Facts on File, 2007).

Morgan, Sally. *From Greek Atoms to Quarks: Discovering Atoms* (Heinemann, 2008).

Silverstein, Alvin, et al. *Matter* (Twenty-First Century, 2009).

Stille, D.R. *Physical Change: Reshaping Matter* (Compass Point, 2006).

Index

A

air resistance, 39
allowed orbits, 16
antimatter, 62–64
antiparticles, 63–64
atomic bombs, 50–51
atomic mass units
    (amu), 48
atomic number, 17–18
atoms
    basic properties of,
      17–20
    in compounds and
      mixtures, 20–23
    electrical forces in,
      15–16
    explanation of,
      10–14, 58
    parts of, 14–17

B

binding energy, 48
boiling point, 33
bosons, 60–62
Broglie, Louis de, 54

C

classical mechanics, 40
compounds, 20–23

conservation of energy,
    law of the, 46, 49
conservation of mass, law
    of the, 47, 49
conservation of mass-
    energy, law of the,
    49, 64
cosmic rays, 58, 60
covalent bonds, 21
crystalline solids/crystals,
    30–32, 33, 55

D

dark matter, 54, 61
Dirac, P.A.M., 62

E

Einstein, Albert, 44, 47,
    50, 52, 54
electromagnetic force,
    40, 62
electron microscope, 58
electrons, 10, 14–17, 18,
    20, 21, 22–23, 28, 29,
    55, 58, 60, 62–63,
    64, 66
elementary particles, 12,
    17, 58, 60, 65
elements, synthesized, 20

evaporation/
    vaporization, 33

F

Fermi, Enrico, 58, 60
freezing point, 33
friction, 39
Frisch, Otto, 50

G

Galileo, 40
gases, 24, 25, 26, 27–29,
    29–30, 33–35
gravitation/gravity, 16, 36,
    40–43, 50, 54, 61, 65

H

Hahn, Otto, 50
Higgs boson, 66–67
hydrogen bomb, 51

I

inertia, 36–39
intermolecular attractive
    forces, 30, 32, 33–35
ionic bonds, 23

ionization, 23
ions, 10, 12, 15–16, 18,
    20, 23
isotopes, 14, 18, 19–20

L

leptons, 60
light microscopes, 58
liquids, 24, 25, 26, 29–30,
    32–33, 35

M

mass
    explanation/definition
        of, 37, 40
    variability of, 45–46
    vs. weight, 43
matter
    equivalence of energy,
        44–49
    explanation/definition
        of, 10, 36, 58
    particle and wave
        properties of, 54–58
    states of, 24–35
matter, states of
    atomic theory and,
        29–32
    explanation of, 24–25
    phase changes, 32–35

solids, liquids, and
gases, 25–29
Meitner, Lise, 50
melting point, 32, 33
mixtures, 20, 23
molecules, 10, 12, 20–21,
22, 23, 29–35, 39,
48–49, 57
motion, laws of, 36, 40
muon, 60

N

neutrinos, 58–60
neutrons, 14–17, 18–19, 48,
57, 58, 60, 61
Newton, Isaac, 36, 50, 52
nuclear fission, 50–51
nuclear fusion bomb
(hydrogen bomb), 51
nuclear reactors, 20, 51
nuclear weapons, 50–51
nucleus, 14–17, 18–19, 20,
29, 40, 48, 50

P

particle accelerators
(atom smashers), 20,
46, 60, 66, 67
Pauli, Wolfgang, 58, 60
photons, 54, 58, 60,
62, 66

plasmas, 28–29
positron, 63, 64
protons, 14–17, 17–19,
48, 57, 58, 60, 61

Q

quantum mechanics,
52, 65
quarks, 17, 60, 66

R

radioactivity, 19–20,
40, 58
relativity, theories of,
44–45, 47, 50, 52
rest mass, 45

S

solids, 24–25, 26, 29–32,
33, 35
solutions, 23
special relativity, theory
of, 44–45, 47, 52
Strassmann, Fritz, 50
string theory,
65–66
strong force, 40
subatomic particles,
14, 17, 60, 64
sublimation, 35
surface tension, 33

T

tau, 60
thermal/heat energy, 30,
    31–32, 33

U

unified field theory (theory
    of everything), 66

V

vaporization/
    evaporation, 33

W

weak force, 38
weight, 43